Long May She Wave

The True Story of Caroline Pickersgill and Her Star-Spangled Creation

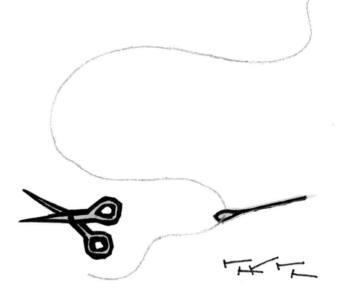

By Kristen Fulton

Illustrated by Holly Berry

Margaret K. McElderry Books
New York London Toronto Sydney New Delhi

Over, under.

THIRTEEN-YEAR-OLD Caroline Pickersgill
stitched three-hundred-fifty-thousand tiny weaves.
She came from a family of the best flag makers.

Open,
close.

Caroline's mother snipped four hundred yards of fabric. She had trouble fitting the six-pointed stars onto the blue square. With a slice from the scissors, she created a five-pointed star that nestled in perfect rows.

Press,
lift.

Caroline's grandmother ironed fifteen stars,

each more than two feet wide.

She had made George Washington's first flag when he fought during the American Revolutionary War.

In 1812, America went to war again with the British. For a year they fought. For a year the British **bombed,** **burned,** and **blasted** their way through the new country.

Preparing for the worst, colonels and generals from Fort McHenry
at Baltimore's harbor asked Caroline and her mother to make a flag so
large that the British could see it from miles away.

For six weeks, Caroline stitched her first flag.

Roll, push.

She worked beside her mother and grandmother. But this flag was so large that all of the seamstresses in the house were called to help.

Flip, pull.

Caroline's cousins Eliza and Margaret Young, as well as Grace Wisher, a thirteen-year-old indentured servant, toiled through the hot days and nights, snipping and sewing.

After she stitched the last stitch, Caroline watched American soldiers raise her flag up the flagpole at Fort McHenry.

For a year, Caroline's flag whipped in the wind.
Would anyone doubt that this was America with a flag so large?

But then something happened. Caroline's world changed, as smoke billowed in the air. The British soldiers had burned Washington, DC.

Now rumors spread like wildfire that the British
were headed to Fort McHenry.
Could it be true?

In the dawn's early light, on September 12, 1814, Caroline woke from her sleep. Shuffling to the window, she looked out over Baltimore. The streets were bare, the homes were empty, and the silence was deafening.

The British were close to Baltimore.

Neighbors who had once proudly hailed the flag and pledged to defend the United States fled.

But Caroline stayed. The flag that she sewed was more than red, white, and blue. It was a symbol of this new nation, the United States.

At the twilight's last gleaming, British ships sailed into the harbor. Banding together, they formed a battery of cannons pointing toward the fort at the southern tip of Baltimore.

Early the next morning, the silence surrounding Caroline's house broke.

The British admiral ordered the American soldiers to take down those broad stripes and bright stars.

Fort McHenry prepared for their perilous fight.

Caroline heard the tapping from snare drums. She listened to the loud tooting from bugle players. Thumping from horse hooves echoed through her Baltimore streets.

Over the ramparts, American soldiers watched the flag curl in the muggy morning air.

BANG!

Caroline searched the bay—her flag was gallantly streaming.

BOOM!

The rockets' red glare lit up the sky from morning till night.

Bombs bursting in air rained over the British fleet.

Each explosion gave enough light for Caroline to see, through the night, that the flag was still there.

After twenty-five hours the last cannon fired, and silence returned.
Peering out her window, Caroline waited for the smoke to clear.
She had to know: Did that star-spangled banner still wave?

Would America still be the land of the free?

When the swirling dust and debris
finally settled, Caroline saw it.

Her first flag, waving good-bye to the British, who
were leaving *the home of the brave.*

AUTHOR'S NOTE

CAROLINE PICKERSGILL'S FATHER passed away when she was just four years old, leaving her mother, Mary, with no income. This was a huge problem at that time, since women did not work outside the home, nor did they own businesses. Caroline's mother defied public opinion and began making and selling flags out of their rented Baltimore, Maryland, home. Eventually she saved enough money to purchase the home and advertise her business—Pickersgill Flags and Ensigns. The Pickersgill flag business was booming, and Mary Pickersgill used this newfound success to reach out to women and young girls who didn't have support from a man. Soon the Pickersgill home was overflowing with females of all ages. Some were learning to be seamstresses while others learned to cook.

Around 1810, a young African American woman by the name of Jenny Wisher approached Mary Pickersgill. Jenny wanted her ten-year-old daughter Grace to learn the skills of a seamstress, and so Jenny contracted Grace as a servant to the Pickersgills.

Unfortunately, during this time in history the lives of African Americans were not consistently documented. Very little is known about Jenny Wisher or about Grace Wisher, the young African American girl who helped to sew the Star-Spangled Banner.

But this story would not be complete without acknowledging everyone who brought the Star-Spangled Banner to life. There were more than the six women and girls who did the actual sewing and assembling of the flag. There were orphans, immigrants, indentured servants, and freed slaves who cooked, farmed the small garden, cleaned, and worked on other flag and signal orders so that Caroline and the other five ladies could sew a flag large enough that the British would see it from miles away. As a team these women brought forth the flag that we hold dear—women who didn't have the right to vote and weren't supposed to work outside the home, own property, own a business, or make contractual decisions.

Prior to the Star-Spangled Banner, Caroline had been in charge of making cavalry banners and bunting for troops. But the flag for Fort McHenry was so large, it required a nimble girl able to get on the floor to puzzle and stitch the large pieces together. Caroline was just the girl. Her first stitches on a flag were for the most historical flag in U.S. history.

As Caroline watched her flag wave throughout the bombing, a young American lawyer being held hostage on a British ship watched the same flag and wrote a poem, "Defense of Fort M'Henry." The lawyer was Francis Scott Key. And today that poem is our national anthem.

Caroline's flag can be viewed at the National Museum of American History in Washington, DC.

SOURCES

Smithsonian Institution, National Museum of American History.

Pingry, Patricia A. *The Story of "The Star-Spangled Banner."* Franklin, TN: Candy Cane Press, 2005.

Kroll, Steven. *By the Dawn's Early Light: The Story of the Star-Spangled Banner.* New York: Scholastic Press, 2000.

Hoose, Phillip M. *We Were There, Too!: Young People in U.S. History.* New York: Farrar, Straus and Giroux, 2001.

Bartoletti, Susan Campbell. *The Flag Maker.* New York: Houghton Mifflin Books for Children, 2004.

The Star-Spangled Banner

O say can you see, by the dawn's early light,

What so proudly we hail'd at the twilight's last gleaming,

Whose broad stripes and bright stars through the perilous fight,

O'er the ramparts we watch'd, were so gallantly streaming?

And the rocket's red glare, the bombs bursting in air,

Gave proof through the night that our flag was still there,

O say does that star-spangled banner yet wave

O'er the land of the free and the home of the brave?

On the shore dimly seen through the mists of the deep,

Where the foe's haughty host in dread silence reposes,

What is that which the breeze, o'er the towering steep,

As it fitfully blows, half conceals, half discloses?

Now it catches the gleam of the morning's first beam,

In full glory reflected now shines in the stream,

'Tis the star-spangled banner—O long may it wave

O'er the land of the free and the home of the brave!

And where is that band who so vauntingly swore,

That the havoc of war and the battle's confusion

A home and a country should leave us no more?

Their blood has wash'd out their foul footsteps' pollution.

No refuge could save the hireling and slave

From the terror of flight or the gloom of the grave,

And the star-spangled banner in triumph doth wave

O'er the land of the free and the home of the brave.

O thus be it ever when freemen shall stand

Between their lov'd home and the war's desolation!

Blest with vict'ry and peace, may the heav'n rescued land

Praise the power that hath made and preserv'd us a nation!

Then conquer we must, when our cause it is just,

And this be our motto—"In God is our trust."

And the star-spangled banner in triumph shall wave

O'er the land of the free and the home of the brave.